Ladybird Picture Books

Indoor Things

Outdoor Things

Things That Go

Things to Wear

Things to Play With

LADYBIRD BOOKS, INC.
Auburn, Maine 04210 U.S.A.
© LADYBIRD BOOKS LTD MCMLXXXVIII
Loughborough, Leicestershire, England

Printed in England

Indoor Things

Illustrated by **Meryl Henderson**

Ladybird Books

red

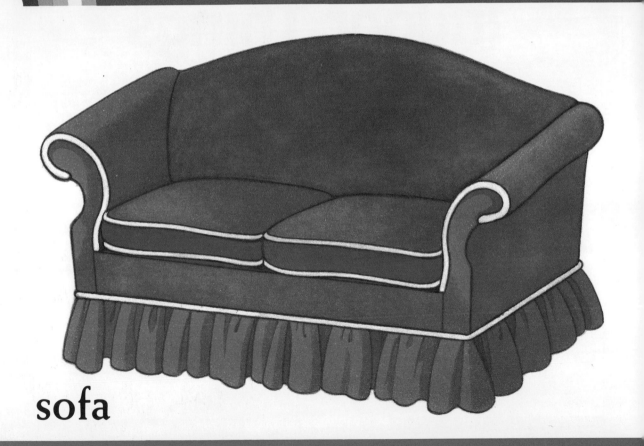

sofa

telephone

rug

teapot

orange

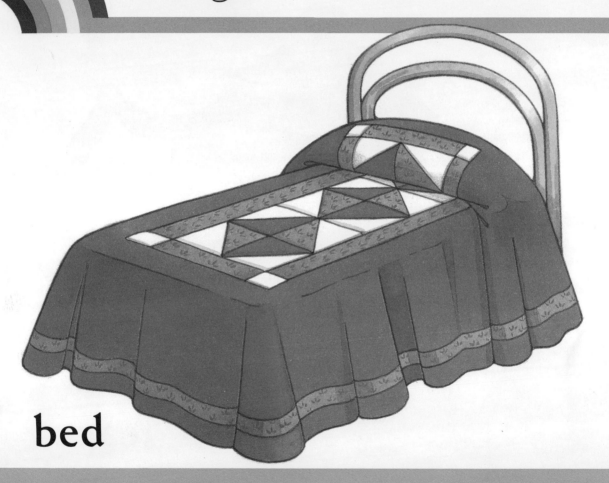

bed

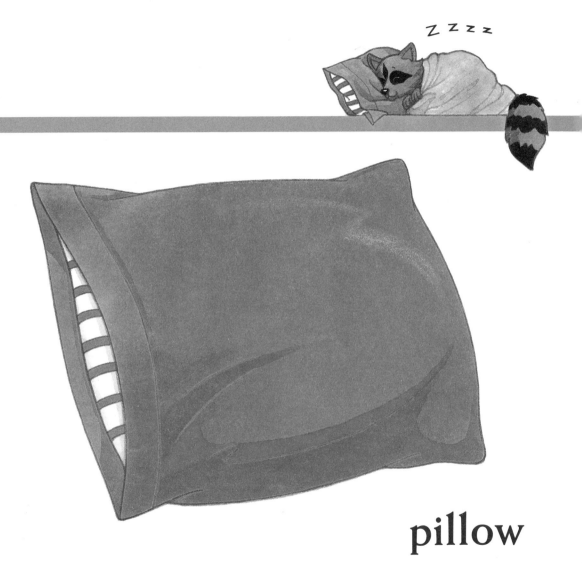

pillow

laundry basket

radio

yellow

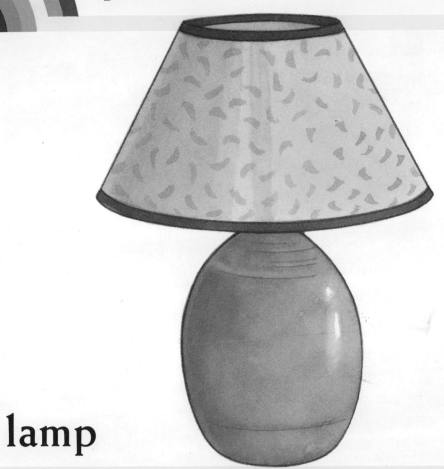

lamp

broom

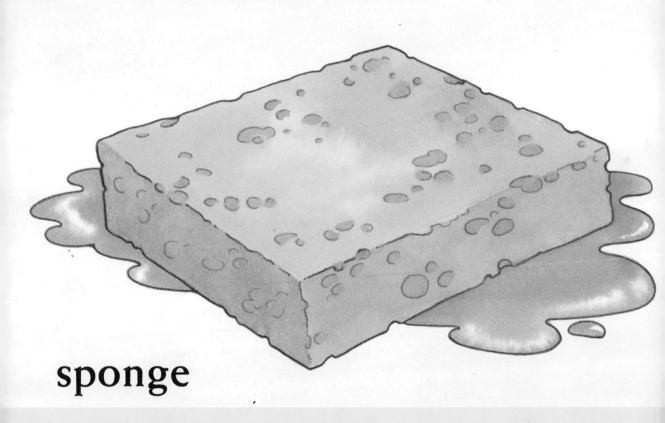

sponge

toy chest

green

mirror

towel

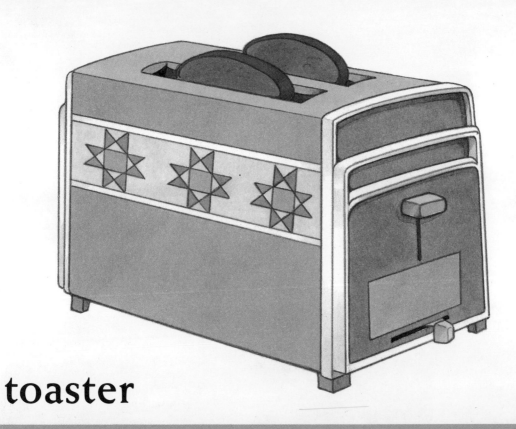

toaster

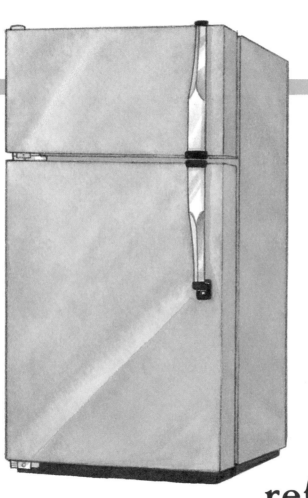

refrigerator

blue

sink

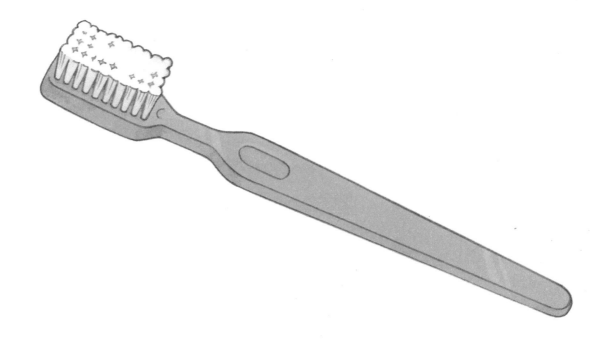

toothbrush

chair

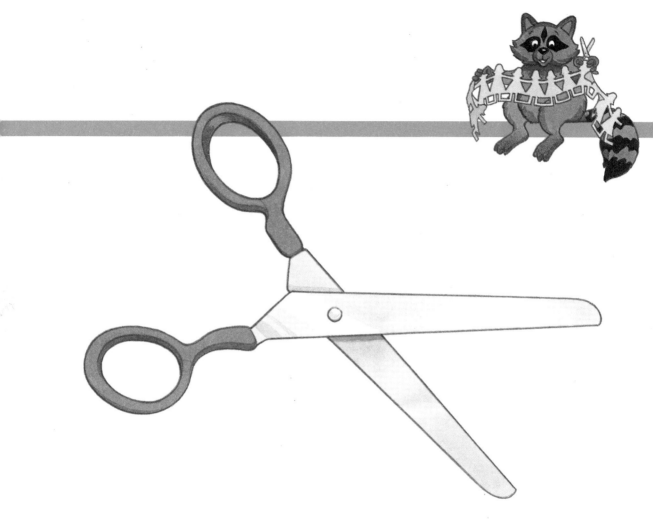

scissors

purple

table

vase

mug

clock